DAVID GAT

It's me again
Lord

PRAYERS FOR TEENAGERS

Kevin
Mayhew

First published in 2002 by
KEVIN MAYHEW LTD
Buxhall, Stowmarket,
Suffolk, IP14 3BW
E-mail: info@kevinmayhewltd.com

9 8 7 6 5 4 3 2 1

ISBN 1 84003 868 3
Catalogue No. 1500486

Cover design by Angela Selfe
Edited and typeset by Elisabeth Bates
Printed and bound in Great Britain

Contents

Foreword

Forewords often get in the way – after all, who reads them anyway? I know I don't. But if you are reading this then I guess I'd better write something.

Prayer isn't a big deal. It was never meant to be. It's not something that is supposed to involve lots of screaming and crying and kneeling and all that kind of stuff. And neither is it just about the big stuff like famine and war and disease. Prayer is nothing more and nothing less than a chat with the Creator. A Creator who makes it quite clear that he's very interested in everything about you. And that means everything. From spots to snogging, sleeping in, exams, even watching telly.

Prayer is our way of sharing everything that we are, everything that we do, everything that we think, everything that we believe – right or wrong, with our God. That's what this book is about really. Just a few ideas of what you can pray to God about. Maybe they'll help. Maybe they'll make you laugh. Maybe they'll spark off new prayers in you. But whatever it gets used for – even if it is just somewhere to rest your coffee on your bedside cabinet – the main thing to remember is that prayer is just about you and God. That's where it begins and that's where it continues from. Sit, kick back, relax, and just chat – it's that simple.

DAVE GATWARD

For . . .

anyone who's ever sat in a Geography lesson on a hot summer's day and thought, 'There must be more to life than this . . .'

. . . and Su, who makes the best sandwiches in the world.

Prayer

Lord . . .
Jesus . . .
God . . .
Father . . .
Help?

I'm having trouble with praying.
I don't really know how to do it.
I don't know what to say,
  what to talk about,
  what to think.

Is there a rule book somewhere, Lord?
OK, I've read your prayer,
  know it off by heart,
  but there's more to it than that, I'm sure.
There must be.
But I'm not sure I've got it right just yet.

The worst thing is trying to keep my mind
  on talking to you.
It'd be easier if I could see you.
If you're talking to a mate
  they're either in front of you
  or on the phone
  or sending an e-mail.
There's evidence that the other person is joining in.

When I speak to you
   all I seem to hear is my voice
   rattling around in my head.
And before too long
   I'm watching telly,
   putting on a CD,
   playing a computer game,
   asleep.

Prayer's not easy.
Sometimes I can just rattle on for ages
   telling you about my day.
Other times I'm just not interested.
Then there are times
   when I don't think I need to say anything
   and yet I feel like I've prayed.
Then there's others when I think I need to say a lot,
   don't know where to start
   and give up.

Did you find it hard, Lord?
Was prayer ever difficult for you?
Do you understand what I'm on about?

You see,
   even this isn't making much sense, is it?
I'm just rambling,
   talking about nothing in particular
   hoping it makes sense to you
   when it doesn't really make sense to me.
Ever.

Do you understand me, Lord?
Do I ever make sense?
Are there times when you just decide to switch off,
    not listen,
    because the words you hear
    don't seem to go anywhere?

Sometimes, Lord,
    I try really, really, hard.
I try to get it right.
I sit down in the quiet,
    read a bit of the Bible,
    think about it, then pray a bit . . .
    and fall asleep.

Then other times, Lord,
    when I'm out,
    I just find myself saying stuff,
    chatting in my mind
    as I walk down the street to the shops.
No preparation,
    no Bible,
    just me.

Prayer,
    it doesn't make sense.
There don't seem to be any rules.
In some ways I like that –
    rules are for breaking
    and if there aren't any
    then it's fairly difficult to go wrong.

A sense of freedom.
But then why would there be rules?
All you ask is that we talk to you,
    speak to you,
    chat with you,
    share our lives with you.
Just like we would with any other friend.

You seem to be interested in the little bits of our lives
    as well as the big bits.
The highs as well as the lows.
Perhaps that's why I find prayer difficult.
I can't really believe
    that you're all that interested
    in me.
Who I am.
What I'm about.
What I'm doing.

Lord,
    as I try to work my way through life,
    as I try to understand what I'm about,
    what I'm for
    as I try to get a grip on this whole praying thing,
    I ask just one thing
    don't get bored with me, Lord.

Amen.

Life and puddles

Lord,
   this is it.
First day back after a summer of freedom.
I can't say I'm all that happy about it, really.
The summer's been great.
Hanging out with mates,
   watching TV,
   getting up late,
   earning some extra cash.
Just kicking back and being me.

Now it's back to school.
A place where the me I like
   often gets shrouded
   by the me I have to be.
It's all about achieving this
   and passing that
   and revising this
   and getting graded for that.

Lord,
   there are so many decisions to make.
Decisions I've spent the whole summer avoiding.
Decisions I simply don't have the answers to.
I've no idea what I really want to do
   or be, or become.
And yet I'm expected to have the answers
   at my fingertips.

Life seems to be getting harder by the minute, Lord.
Gone are the days when the biggest decision I had to make
    was what mud to throw where,
    what puddle to jump in
    or which tree to climb.
I miss those days, Lord.
They were fun, exciting,
    full of imagination, freedom.

But then, why should it be any different now?
Why should these questions and decisions
    tie me down?
Maybe, Lord, they shouldn't.
I've got some control of what goes on.
If I think about it properly,
    I guess making these decisions could be
    equally fun, exciting,
    full of imagination, freedom.

I'm older,
    the playground is bigger,
    and that means more stuff to do,
    more fun to have,
    more things to explore.

Perhaps, Lord
    life is simply a really big puddle
    just waiting to be jumped into!
    Help me put my wellies on, Lord.

Amen.

Argh!

Lord,
    er...
    well...
    how do I put this...
    erm...
    I don't really know how to...
    look, it goes something like this:

    AAAAAAAAAAAAAAAAAAAA
    AAAAAAAAAAAAAAAAAAAA
    AAAAAAAAAAAAAAAAAAAA
    AAAAAAAAAAAAAAAAAAAA
    AAAAAAAAAAAAAAAAAAAA
    AAAAAAAAAAAAAAAAAAAA
    AAAAAAAAAAAAAAAAAAAA
    AAAAAAAAAAAAAAAAAAAA
    AAAAAAAAAAAAAAAAAAAA
    AAAAAAAAAAARGH!!!!!!!!!!!!

Sometimes, Lord,
    that's all I can think to say.
When my head feels like it's going to explode,
    when I want to lash out,
    rip down all my posters,
    break all my CDs,
    pull my hair out...

it's at these times
that all I can do is scream.

I don't have any words to express how I feel,
    no poems or carefully chosen sentences.
Words suddenly lose all meaning
    and all I want to do,
    all that will help
    is to scream
    and scream
    and scream
    until I can't scream any more.

And that's it, Lord.
I just wanted to let you know
    that that's how I feel
    right now
    at this very minute –
    like I could scream the world into a pile of rubble.

Amen.

Sick of it all

I've had enough, Lord.
I'm sick of it.
Of this,
    of that,
    of them,
    of you.

I'm sick of my life,
    what I'm doing with it
    and what everyone else
    keeps telling me I should do with it.

I'm sick of Monday to Sunday,
    of weeks and months and years.
I'm sick of telly and breakfast
    and last night's rubbish film
    at the cinema.

I'm sick of my parents,
    my family and what I'm supposed to do
    at the weekend.
I'm sick of my clothes and my hair
    and everyone I know.

And now I'm sitting here,
    sick of sitting here,
    talking to you,
    because I've got no one else who'll understand
    just why I am sick of it all.

People ask what's up,
   if I'm all right,
   what's wrong.
But I don't have any answers.
I just feel awful,
   rubbish,
   tired,
   depressed,
   nasty,
   lonely,
   sad.

Nothing makes sense;
   the way I feel, the way I am,
   the way I behave, the things I do.
I always seem to upset people
   or annoy them.

I'm sick of being the me that I am
   and the me that I seem to be more and more.
Growing up is supposed to be fun,
   challenging,
   but it's not at the moment.
I feel . . .
   sick of it.

Do you understand, Lord?
Do you ever get sick of it?
I can't believe that you don't.
You know, when you get that feeling

that it seems like it'd be a good idea
just to throw the towel in,
pack up
and walk out in to the world,
leave everything behind
and not look back;
to live a life of having been forgotten.
Sometimes, Lord,
    that's the thing I want to do more than anything.
Run away,
    get away,
    disappear.

And then I think to myself
    about what it'd be like,
    and it'd be just like it is now
    but without my friends
    and my family
    whom I'm sick of
    and who, I'm sure, are sick of me
    but still stick with me,
    by my side.

Amazing thought, that, Lord.
My friends and family putting up with me
    when I'm like this.
    I know I wouldn't.
    I know I don't.

There are no reasons, Lord,
    no explanation for why I feel the way I do.

It just sometimes happens
   and I feel rubbish
   and end up talking to you
   just because I can.
Because it's the only thing
   I'm not sick of.
Ever.

Amen.

I'm sorry

Lord,
   I'm sorry.
I made a mess of something today
   and I'm sorry.

I don't know how it happened
   but things seemed to get a little out of control.
I said some things I didn't mean
   and upset someone.
I wasn't very nice at all.
Actually, Lord,
   I'm embarrassed.

Why did I do it, Lord?
What was I on?
What got into me?
One minute I was me,
   next I was this . . .
   this . . .
   this mouthy idiot upsetting people because he could.

I wish I'd controlled myself.
I wish I'd kept my mouth shut.
I wish I could change what I've done.

I'm going to say sorry, Lord.
That's why I'm praying now.

I'm off to see the person I upset
   and say sorry.
Not that they'll believe I'm sorry –
   I know I wouldn't.
But I've got to, Lord.
And that's why I'm praying,
   because saying sorry
   always seems so hard,
   so difficult.

I don't like admitting when I'm wrong,
   when I've been bad.
It just seems to rub it in.
But I'm going to, Lord.
I'm going to do it
   and learn from it
   and hopefully not be such an idiot again.

Help me, Lord.

Amen.

Being a Christian

Lord,
    I'm not very good at believing in you.
At home, on my own,
    it's easy.
At school,
    surrounded by people,
    it isn't.
I haven't got any answers,
    I haven't got any proof.
And if one thing's for sure,
    I'm certainly not brave enough
    to say I believe in you
    and pray.

I feel really rubbish, Lord,
    like I'm the only person like this.
But that can't be true, can it?

I want to be able to talk about you
    confidently, freely,
    with a smile on my face!
I don't want to sort of mumble
    or just stay silent.

Lord,
    you're an important part of who and what I am.
    I talk to you all the time,
    you help me get through each day.

You're with me at school,
   home,
   everywhere.
And yet talking about you to others
   is a nightmare.

I don't know why, Lord.
Perhaps there's something wrong with me.
But, at the same time,
   I know there isn't.
I'm just me
   and I'm just scared.
I don't want to be alienated,
   bullied,
   laughed at.
That's only normal, isn't it?

Do you understand, Lord?
You must've felt like this.
It's not easy, is it?
But then you had so much more to deal with.
Me?
Just a few people at school.
But it's still terrifying.

I know there's no answer, Lord,
   and I know I'm not going to suddenly turn into
   a really confident
   'talking about God brilliantly' person.
And in some respects I don't want to.

A few people have asked about why I go to church
   and I've told them.
Some have asked if I pray
   and I've said yes.
So maybe I am doing something.
Maybe it's not about being someone I'm not,
   but about just being me.
Is that it, Lord?

Wow! An answer in the middle of me praying!
Amazing, Lord!

Amen.

Why don't they understand?

Lord?
Why don't they understand?
My parents, I mean.
Mum just went mental because of what I was wearing.
What's wrong with it?
I look so cool.
I look great.
She just doesn't get it.
She can't do.
And anyway,
    what's so wrong with asking for a tattoo?

Maybe I was pushing it a bit far,
    but someone at school's got one.
I've seen it – it's fantastic.
Really totally great.
I want one.
Mum doesn't quite agree
    and neither does Dad.

They seem to think I'm doing this on purpose,
    just to annoy them,
    to freak them out,
    scare them.
But I'm not.
This is who I am and what I want to look like.
What's so wrong with that?

Maybe I should have asked
   before I dyed my hair,
   and cleaned the sink a little better
   to get rid of the dye,
   but there's still no need to go mental at me, is there?

I sometimes wonder if my parents will ever understand me.
Or if they even want to.
All they seem to do at the moment
   is stop me doing what I want to,
   and that doesn't seem very fair.
I'm nearly an adult now,
   I should have a bit more freedom.
Everyone else at school does.
Or at least seems to.

Maybe it was a bit thoughtless
   to cut the bottoms off my new jeans, Lord.
Should have asked really, or used an old pair.
And perhaps, if I'd asked for Mum's help,
   I wouldn't have dyed my hair and half my forehead, too.

Sometimes, Lord,
   I just don't make any sense,
   not even to me.

I hope I make sense to you, Lord.

Amen.

Being old

Lord,
   I can't imagine being old.
It seems almost impossible
   that I may well one day
   be old.
Old enough to forget where I've left my teeth.

It's a frightening thought, Lord.
It scares me.
Not least because I know that when I'm old
   I'll be very close to dying,
   and no matter what I believe,
   that's still very scary.

Is this a daft thing to think, Lord?
Hope not.
Because I think it quite a lot.
The weird thing is that I feel now
   like I did five years ago.
I'm older, but I'm still me.
That means I'll still be me when I'm really old,
   and I'll probably remember thinking this
   when I was young.

What's being old like, Lord?
Is it OK?
Is it painful?

Is it scary?
Or is it like the rest of our life;
  exciting, scary,
  dull, weird, confusing,
  sad, brilliant . . .

I'm a teenager scared of growing old, Lord.
I'm a teenager with a lot on my mind.
I'm me wondering what I'll be like when I'm 94.
I'm me, Lord,
  just me,
  and when I'm old I'll probably say the same.

So I guess, Lord,
  that this is just me
  planning ahead,
  hoping that when I am old
  you'll look after me,
  hold me,
  and help me deal with any of the fears
  I have now
  that may still
  be hanging around.

Amen.

Failed again

Lord,
  I'm rubbish.
I hate school,
  I hate the lessons,
  I hate the teachers,
  I hate the exams
  and I hate the fact
  that I just failed.
Again.

Why do we have to take exams?
They're pointless, Lord.
And what use is physics anyway?
Why do I need to know
  all about kinetic energy
  and other stuff I don't quite get yet?

I seem to be the only one struggling, Lord.
Everyone else seems to understand what they're doing.
Everyone seems to find it easy.
Everyone except me.
Mum and Dad try to convince me that it's important,
  that I need to try harder,
  succeed.
I've got to think about my career, apparently.

My career, Lord.
What will that be?

Why don't I know yet?
How can I do exams for a future I haven't got a clue about?
It doesn't make sense.
Physics doesn't make sense.
I don't make sense.

I hate failing, Lord.
I hate doing badly.
Sometimes though, Lord,
    it's not that I haven't tried,
    it's just that I don't understand,
    and sometimes I think that my teachers,
    my friends,
    my parents,
    don't understand that.
Trying harder doesn't always make that much difference.

I want to do well, Lord,
    to be the best I can be,
    and I'm not giving up.
Just the pressure, Lord,
    the pressure to do well, to pass,
    sometimes overwhelms me
    and the only one I can turn to,
    talk to,
    cry to,
    is you.

Amen.

Breaking up

Lord,
   this is going to be quick
   because I don't really know what to pray,
   but I need your help.
I'm going to break up with you-know-who
   and I don't really know how to do it.
I'm scared,
   nervous,
    sad.

It's a shame, Lord,
   because we've had some great fun together.
I don't really know why I'm finishing it.
I just know it's something I've got to do.
It'll hurt us both, Lord,
   and I guess I'll be in the bad books for a while.
Hopefully we'll get over it,
   move on.

It'll be difficult when one of us ends up
   going out with someone else, I know that, Lord.
But that's all part of it.
Doesn't make it any easier though.

Right, here goes,
   better go round and do the deed.
Be with us both, Lord.

Amen.

Valentine's Day

Today, Lord,
  is about as much fun
  as walking on broken bottles.
It's all very well if you're going out with someone,
  but if you're not –
  and I'm not –
  it's just a day of being made to feel really low.

People at school brandish their valentine's cards
  like medals of honour
  and I feel like someone
  who never even got to see
  the battlefield.
There are badges and teddy bears
  and boxes of chocolates
  all over the place
  and none of them are mine.
Not fair, Lord,
  not fair.

I did send one though, Lord.
I guess they received it,
  but now I'm beginning to wonder why I bothered.
It's not as if they'll ever know it was from me.
A bit pointless really.
Still, at least it'll make them feel good.
Wish I knew what that felt like, Lord.

Is it stupid to want a Valentine's card, Lord?
Is it?
I feel stupid.
I feel really, really stupid.
But I still want one.
Just to know that someone, somewhere,
    doesn't think I'm all that bad.

Know what I mean, Lord?
Hope so.

Amen.

Childhood

Hi, Lord.
Just been looking through some old photos.
There are some really daft ones of me,
    and the clothes I had to wear.
What were my parents on, Lord?

It's odd looking back.
I don't feel old at all,
    yet these pictures are of a me
    and that seems so long ago.

I remember when I was younger,
    thinking how far away the rest of my life seemed.
It felt like I'd be young for ever.
That making dens under the bed,
    playing in the garden,
    enjoying the box more than the toy,
    would be an eternity.

Now here I am,
    only a few years older really,
    and everything's changed so much.
My mind doesn't seem to get a chance
    to think about the simple things in life anymore.
It's all about doing this, that and the other
    so that everything will be OK tomorrow.

It's all about doing something for my future,
   achieving something,
   working hard.

The play element of my life, Lord,
   has been replaced by the work, work, work
   of school, homework and more school.
Everyone wants me to do well,
   to make something of myself,
   not to waste what I've got.

Looking at the me I used to be
   and thinking of the me now,
   we seem so different.
Yet, Lord,
   I still feel like that person.
I can remember what it was like –
   when wading in the shallows of a lake
   would mean waves would swamp my wellies.
When a weekend was nothing more
   than an excuse to run around,
   get dirty,
   ride a bike,
   make a catapult
   and then come home for Mum's meat pie
   with chips and peas.

The me of then is important, Lord.
   I don't want to lose touch with who I was.
What I did then,

what I do now;
  it's all me, who I am.
Yes, I have to push myself,
  work hard,
  but I can only do that
  if I hold on to exactly who
  and what
  I am.

So, Lord,
  as I look at these pictures
  and daydream my way
  back to ponds and puddles,
  bikes and slides,
  help me not to forget the who that I was
  as I live the me that I am
  and become the person
  you want me
  to be.

Amen.

Bullied

It hurts, Lord,
   on the inside
   as well as on the outside.
Why do they do it?
Why do they pick on me?
I don't even know their names,
   just their voices, their faces,
   the words they use that I can't repeat.

They cornered me today in the cloakroom.
Pushed me around, called me names.
One of them spat at me,
   another pushed me onto the floor.
When they left
   they poured the contents of my bag
   onto my head
   and all I could hear was their laughter.

I want to fight back, Lord,
   but I'm scared to.
There are so many of them and I'm just me.
A nobody.
I must be, to get treated like this.
Worthless.

Why do you let it happen, Lord?
What have I done that's so wrong?

Why me?
It doesn't make sense,
   none of it does.

It makes coming to school hellish.
I'm afraid of the lesson ending.
I can't concentrate on my work.
And that's beginning to show in my results.

Mum and Dad have asked what's wrong,
   but I can't tell them –
   it'd only make it worse.
They'd only come into school
   and then the gang would find out
   and beat me up.
Or worse.

I can't live like this, Lord.
It's just not fair.
It's wrong,
   all of it is wrong.
And where are you in it?
I can't see you,
   I can't feel you,
   I can't hear you.
   I feel so alone.
   It's just me,
  this dark room
  and the dread of tomorrow.

Did you ever feel like this, Lord?
Did you dread tomorrow?
Did you feel afraid
   to the point where the panic makes you feel
   like you're about to explode?

I guess you did,
   but I just don't see why I should
   or what I'm supposed to do about it.
Because I feel trapped
   and exposed
   and helpless.

I'm scared, Lord.

Amen.

Christmas

Lord,
   it's Christmas time again.
And I'm very excited!
I always thought as you got older
   the magic would disappear –
    not so, Lord!
I can't wait!

Best part is the stocking – I love that.
Waking up to find presents in a sock
   lying on my bed.
Then there's the day of laughs,
   food,
   fun,
   more presents.
And it's great seeing the faces of people
   as they open something you've bought them –
I love that bit, Lord!

I admit though, that I do sometimes lose sight
   of what it's all about.
I was out in town last week
   and passed someone lying under a blanket
   in a doorway.
It made me think.
I suddenly felt very guilty
   about being so lucky.

And then I felt completely helpless.
There's me with so much
    and then there are those with so little.
What can I do?

I don't know, Lord.
Perhaps praying about it is at least a start.
But I don't want it to end there.
I actually want to be able to do something,
    change something,
    help this world get a little bit better.

So, Lord,
    as I sit through my Christmas,
    enjoying everything that happens,
    help me not to forget that person in the doorway
    and to try to make a difference.

Amen.

Friendship

Lord,
   it's about friendship.
Don't know why really,
   it just is.
Bear with me.

I've got some fantastic mates, Lord.
Friends I hope will be friends for ever.
We've grown up together,
   explored the world we've lived in together.
Scraped knees,
   climbed trees,
   gone to school,
   danced,
   ridden bikes . . .
And still we're friends, growing together.

I think, Lord,
   that sometimes, that's the best bit about being alive;
   growing up with friends you love to bits.
It's really exciting to watch each other's lives develop.
We're all making different decisions,
   going different ways,
   but we're all in it together.
It's great!

Being a friend isn't always easy,
   but then if it was it wouldn't work.

Friendship is challenging,
   difficult, demanding,
   but that's what makes it so great.

If there's one gift I thank you for, Lord,
   it's the gift of all my friends.
They've added so much to my life,
   given me so much,
   made me laugh so many times;
   the memories are so real, vivid.
Often, if I'm feeling low,
I just rewind some of these memories
   and replay them in my mind,
   and I smile.

I've learnt so much from my friends,
   they've been there when I've been down
   and picked me up.
They've encouraged me to do things
   I never thought I was capable of.

It's an amazing thing, friendship, Lord.
And all I want to do
   is sit here
   and say thank you
   and hope that I will continue to be as good a friend to them
   as they are to me.

Thanks for my friends, Lord.

Amen.

Death

Lord,
    our dog died today
    and I cried.
It was awful.
One minute she was fine,
    next minute she wasn't.
We had to call the vet
    and she was put down.
We all cried, Lord,
    even Dad.

I don't think I've ever felt so sad, Lord.
It was as though a close friend had died,
    but then that's actually what happened.
We'd grown up together,
    played,
    run around,
    slept on the sofa,
    watched telly,
    gone for walks.
Our lives were a part of each other.
And now she's gone and already the house is empty.

I don't think I ever really expected her to die, Lord.
Friendship's like that – it feels immortal.
I secretly hoped she'd live for ever.

I'm praying about the death of our pet dog, Lord.
I feel daft doing it,
    but I need to.
I'm sad,
    I miss her,
    and sometimes just telling you makes me feel better.

Thanks, Lord.

Amen.

Zits

I've got spots, Lord.
Loads of them.
I've got them on my forehead,
    my nose,
    my chin,
    my cheeks;
    there are some in my ears
    and now I'm getting them on my back.
Being a teenager stinks, Lord.

I'm trying yet another cream to get rid of them,
    but it isn't working.
And why is it that I'm the only one in our year
    who's got acne?
Where's everyone else's spots?
Why is it only me who's been cursed?

Some people laugh at me, Lord,
    call me names.
I wish they had spots, Lord.
Then they'd leave me alone.

Apparently it's what's on the inside that counts,
    but, Lord, looking like this,
    feeling the way I do,
    I find that hard to believe.
I look dreadful.
I think I might grow my hair to hide them.

When do they go, Lord?
When will I look normal?
When will I have a complexion
    that people will look at and think,
    'Mmmm . . . nice!'
    rather than
    'Oh . . . yuk'?

I want to be attractive,
I want to look good,
    not be like this.
I know you can't magic them away, Lord,
    make them disappear at night,
    but,
    if you've got time to spare,
    could you help other people see past the spots
    and see the real me?

Amen.

Why didn't you stop it?

Lord, they went too far today.
I was in the toilets
   when they came in.
One pushed me,
   another took my bag
   and another made sure no one else was looking.
Then they all grabbed me and . . .

Lord,
   I can't say it.
   I can't go into it.
You know what happened.
You were there.
So why didn't you help me?
Why didn't you stop it?
If you're everywhere then where were you today?
Where were you?
I was screaming, Lord,
   and no one came.
I was hurting, Lord,
   and no one came.
I was scared, Lord,
   and no one came.

I don't even know why I bother praying any more.
What use is it?
What use is believing in you
   if I'm not even safe at school?

There's no answer, Lord.
Why not?
Why don't you hear me?

I hate my life, Lord.
There's no fun in it any more.
I shouldn't feel like this;
   it's wrong,
    but what else is there to feel?

How do I make all of this go away?
How do I stop it?
I've even considered running away, Lord.
Packing up,
   leaving,
    going anywhere so long as it's not here.

I'm desperate, Lord.
I'm so desperate that I just don't know what to do,
   where to turn,
   who to turn to.

If you are there,
   if you do exist,
   if you do care,
   help me, Lord.

Help me.

Amen.

Decisions, decisions

Lord,
    it's me again.
It's that time of year when we get to decide
    exactly
    what we want to do with the rest
    of our lives.
The choices I make now,
    about what I want to do for the next two years,
    will affect every decision,
    everything I do
    from that point on.

I don't want to do it, Lord.
I don't think I'm ready.

It seems daft all this.
Last night I was watching late-night telly
    and today I'm altering my life for good.
And tomorrow there'll be nothing I can do about it.
That's a scary thought, Lord.

I've been wondering for a while, Lord,
    hoping,
    that perhaps I'd soon suddenly realise
    why I was here,
    what I wanted to do with 'me'
    and then just do it.

It seems, Lord, that this was wishful thinking.
I've got as much idea about that
    as I have about how to approach you-know-who
    about you-know-what.
(Teenage romance, Lord: it's rubbish.)

What do I want to do with my life, Lord?
I dunno.
Haven't a clue.
I want it to be fun, exciting, challenging,
    dangerous, fulfilling, different,
    wild, satisfying, exhilarating . . .
    which leaves me with a great choice:
    the secret service or pro stunt-type person.
Not very sensible really.
Be fun telling Mum, though.

Did you ever get thoughts like this, Lord,
    or did you always know?
There's none of that info in the Bible
    (I've read some of it, seriously)
    and it'd be good to know.

The trouble is –
    everyone else seems to know what they want to do.
Apparently.
And, if what they're saying is true,
    we're going to be overrun with bankers,
    accountants and lawyers.
What an awful thought.

I'm not getting anywhere here, Lord.
I know no more now than I did yesterday
   or the day before
   about what I want to do.
I guess all I can do is hope that whatever choices I make,
   I don't waste them.
After all, Lord,
   that's the last thing I want my life to be:
   a waste.

Amen.

Dreams

Lord,
    I admit it:
    I want to be famous.
I can't help it,
    it's just the way it is.
I want to be famous
    and rich
    and gorgeous
    and rich
    and famous
    and . . .

Does it matter, Lord?
Are these dreams OK?
Is it wrong to wish?
I don't know.
I can't find anything about it in the Bible.

I want to be a pop star,
    with a string of number one hits.
I want to play at Wembley,
    sing to millions,
    appear on children's TV.

I want to be a film star,
    in an action movie where I win against the odds.
I want to be bigger than *Star Wars*,

fly everywhere in a private jet,
have someone write my biography.

Dreams, Lord.
It's all dreams.
But then,
    when someone asks what I want to do with my life,
    I don't have any sensible answers.
I've never thought about becoming this
    or that
    or the other.
A doctor,
    a teacher,
    a surgeon,
    a politician.

Are these thoughts not in my head on purpose?
Everyone else seems to have them,
    or so they say.
Wanting to be a pop star
    doesn't really help when choosing your GCSEs
    or your A levels.
No one takes you seriously.
Not that anyone ever did.

Lord,
    I'm sorry to bother you with this.
I know it's not really all that important –
    me wishing to be famous.
But it's a part of who I am.

And sometimes,
    dreams help to make life
    make sense.
It's the dreams that keep me going,
    dreams of what I could be
    because others have done it too.
And they wouldn't have done it
    if they hadn't dreamt it.

Famous people
    are just people at the end of the day.
The only difference, really,
    is that lots of people know who they are.
That's it.

Maybe it's not the fame I'm after, Lord,
    though it would be nice.
Maybe I just like to think that perhaps,
    one day,
    my life will make sense,
    I will make sense,
    and I will make you proud
    of what I've done.
That's my real dream, Lord.

Amen.

Proof of ID

Lord,
   It's me again.
Last night I was in one of those rebellious moods.
You know the kind, where I think I'm right
   and everyone else is wrong.
Well, I went with a few friends to a pub
   just for a laugh.
One of us went to get the drinks
   and then it was my turn.
I got asked for ID, Lord.
Oddly enough, I didn't have it.
So we all got asked to leave.

Don't really know why I did it, Lord.
I guess this whole growing-up thing's a bit confusing.
I sometimes feel that I want to get it over and done with
   really, really quickly.
I want to be old enough to get served in pubs
   NOW.
I want to be old enough to drive
   NOW.
Know what I mean?

Proof of ID . . .
It made me think, Lord,
   rare I know,
     but if I'm going to be asked to prove my age

I can't help but wonder why you don't produce
just a little proof
of you actually being there.

I was asked at school once to prove you existed;
   proof of God.
I couldn't do it,
   sat silent,
   got laughed at.
Not nice, Lord, not nice.
And, if you don't mind me saying so,
   a little bit pointless, too.
I don't believe in you, just to get picked on
   and laughed at.
I believe in you because I do.
I can't always think of reasons,
   come up with proof,
   evidence.
Actually, Lord,
   I can't ever do that.
Wish I could.

Does this make sense, Lord?
I sit here wondering sometimes if I'm just talking to myself,
   or talking to the air.
Did you ever feel like that?

It's hard this Christian thing, Lord;
   faith's really difficult to deal with
   and at times, impossible.

Deep down I know there's something there,
   that I'm not lying to myself;
   that praying means something,
   does something,
   is heard.
But I guess, Lord,
   like that barman,
   I just occasionally need to see a little ID,
   some proof.

Amen.

Drunk

I shouldn't have done it, Lord,
   I know that.
I should've known better,
   and I do.
But I was curious, Lord,
   and the rebellious side of me took over;
   and now,
   here I am,
   experiencing what I assume to be
   my first hangover.
It's not nice, Lord.

I was round at a mate's
   and the parents were out
   so we raided the drinks cupboard.
Then we had a competition of some sort
   involving drinking if you lost.
Guess who lost, Lord.

I must admit that for a while
   it was rather fun.
The sensation was new and weird
   and very enjoyable.
I didn't even mind the taste that much.
But now, Lord,
   now I feel terrible.
I've already been sick twice

and I'm now lying here,
in bed,
sweating buckets.
I wonder if my parents know?

Lord,
I know it was a daft thing to do,
but sometimes
I can't help but just go
that little bit too far.
The exploring side of me takes over.
It's not a bad thing, Lord,
but I guess I need to control it a little.
Help me do that, Lord.

Amen.

Hide 'n' seek

I've been wondering, Lord;
   is there any chance that I could ever see you?
Is that a stupid question?
Do you mind me asking it?
Hope not.

Anyway,
   you see, the thing is,
   I'm finding it a little hard to grasp
   what you are,
   who you are,
   why you are –
   if you 'are' at all . . .
Make sense?

At school the other day
   someone told someone else
   who told a few others
   that they'd seen me going to church,
   that I was a Bible basher.
They all laughed
   and then started saying things like
   'How can you believe in God if you can't see him?'
   'Prove God exists, then – go on!'
   'If God is real, why is there war in the world?'

I said nothing.
Actually, that's not strictly true.

I said lots of things
   that I'm not proud of,
   that you probably heard
   (assuming you're there . . .)
   and that probably didn't make me a shining example
   of what I'm supposed to be
   if I believe in – and follow – you.

So, Lord,
   I'm after some proof.
Some tangible evidence.
You see, it's not like you're a pop star or anything.
I can't run into school shouting, 'I've seen Jesus!'
   and then 'wow' everyone with a picture of you and me,
   which you've autographed.
That's the kind of evidence people are after.
They want television proof,
   newspaper articles,
   something tangible.

All I was able to give them
   was a string of abuse
   and the view of my back as I walked away,
   confused, upset,
   angry.

I don't want to doubt you, Lord,
   but I do.
I don't want to not believe in you,
   but sometimes I can't help it.

'God is everywhere'
    just isn't enough sometimes.
Actually, a lot of the time.
Is that wrong?
Is that a bad thing?

Lord, this is so confusing.
I'm supposed to believe in something I can't see,
    can't touch,
    can't really explain,
    but for some reason,
    for some insane reason,
    makes sense.
Even though it doesn't to many people.

I'm sorry, Lord.
Maybe it's because I'm young.
Maybe it's because I'm me.
Or maybe it's because I'm human.
I don't really know.
But I do know it's difficult.
Especially when everywhere I go
    I see proof of so many other things.
    TV news of war and famine
    and drug busts
    and people breaking under pressure
    and violence
    and tears
    and terrorism
    and loneliness
    and . . .

See, Lord?
There seems to be so much proof of you not existing.
It's vivid, real,
    in your face.
To so many people,
    even to me,
      proof of your existence just doesn't measure up.

And yet still I'm sitting here,
    talking to you,
    questioning,
    trying to listen.

I guess this is called faith, Lord.
Believing in you,
    seeing you in the world around me,
    knowing you're with me
    even when all the evidence points the other way.

Sometimes it's lonely, Lord,
    believing in you.
But sometimes, Lord,
    just sometimes,
    it makes sense.
Which is why I hold on.
Which is why I never give up.
Which is why I still, occasionally,
    doubt.

Amen.

End of the week

I'm shattered, Lord.
It's been a really busy week.
Loads of work at school,
   loads of work at home,
   and all I've got to look forward to this weekend
   is more of the same.

I need to sleep, Lord,
   to rest a little,
   not think anymore.
But sometimes it's difficult.
Like now:
   my body's tired,
   but my brain's rushing around,
   thinking of things I need to do,
   things I should've done.

It's dark, Lord,
   and the night outside is quiet.
The bed's cool
   and I must remember to take my glasses off
   before I fall asleep.

Watch over me, Lord.

Amen.

Snogging

Lord,
    I don't know how to snog.
I've never snogged.
I've never even been asked out.
Is there something wrong with me?

Snogging looks great, by all accounts.
Everyone who does it certainly seems to enjoy it.
I want to be one of them, Lord.
I want to have a snog.

Do you get many prayers like this, Lord?
About snogging?
I guess so;
    it is a fairly big thing
    on the teenage agenda.
And there's a disco next week as well.
What's it going to be like if I go to that
    and have my first snog
    and it's rubbish
    and the other person goes,
    'Yuk!
    that was rubbish!'
    and then tells everyone?
I'll never get a snog again!
Ever!

Lord,
    it may sound funny,
    but to me,
    in my life,
    now,
    it isn't.
It's the little things like this
    that can really screw you up.
It's not always exams
    and pressure
    and the big future decisions that take a hold,
    but the little everyday things,
    like snogging.

And that's why I'm speaking about it
    to you, Lord.
You want to know me,
    the real me,
    the deep-down me.
And Lord,
    that means you need to hear
    about all my thoughts,
    all my worries,
    all my concerns,
    and right now it's the fact that I've never snogged.
Hope you understand.

Amen.

I failed

Lord,
   I failed.
Everyone else passed,
   except me.

How is this possible?
I'm not stupid.
I revised.
I did the work.
And still I didn't pass.
The teacher wasn't impressed,
   my friends didn't quite know what to say,
   and Mum and Dad
   are being just a little bit too polite about it all.

I feel so stupid.
I feel like an idiot.
I mean, Lord,
   if I'm failing now,
   how am I going to cope in the future?
How am I going to pass anything?
How am I going to get anywhere?

Maybe I'm wasting my time,
   maybe I should just stop right now,
   set my sights nice and low
   and just muddle through.

That's what I feel like doing.
That's what I want to do.
But it's not what I'm going to do.

Lord,
   failure is so hard to deal with.
It feels as though the whole of me is a failure
   rather than the result of just one little exam.
And that can't be true.
I'm more than that result on a piece of paper.
I have to deal with this,
   learn from it,
   move on.

That's easier said than done –
   much easier to put a video on,
   eat crisps,
   cry a bit,
   give up.

I failed this time, Lord,
   but I'm not a failure.
I didn't pass this test,
   but I'm not going to fail the bigger test,
   the test of me making something of what I am.

Failure's scary, Lord,
   it catches you off balance.
But it also makes you think:
   No, I'm not giving up.

I'm going to try harder,
   do better,
      never give up.
Ever.

And I won't, Lord.
I'm not going to let this get to me.
Help me fight back, Lord.

Amen.

Late

I haven't got long, Lord,
    because I'm late
    because I slept in
    and my alarm didn't go off.
So I'm running as fast as I can be bothered
    to my first lesson
    on some ology or other
    and I just thought it'd be worth my while
    to pray to have an ease of entry
    into the class.
The last thing I need
    is to turn up and find Ms 'I'm-the-nasty-teacher'
    sharpening her teeth,
    if you know what I mean.

So, Lord,
    if you wouldn't mind;
    could you pacify her a little,
    or something?
Just enough to get me through the door
    to my seat,
    without too much blood being spilt?

Thanks, Lord –
    and I'll remember to set my alarm tomorrow – promise.

Amen.

Part of the wider picture

I don't care any more, Lord;
   French can take a running jump.
It's not going in
   and I'm not allowed out.
Not fair.

I've grappled with this for years, Lord,
   tried to understand the subject,
   speak sentences that make sense,
   get the verbs right and the past participles
   and all that stuff.
But it just doesn't seem to be clicking.

Tomorrow's our mock exam;
   I have to do my best to sound French
   and I think I've got about as much chance of that
   as I have of becoming a film star.

I've tried my hardest,
   I've done all I can to learn it,
   understand it,
   get to grips with it.
I guess all I can do is my best, Lord.

So,
   when I'm doing the exam, Lord,
   when it's over,

when I get my mark,
help me to look at it
as a part of the wider picture.
This is one exam
in one subject
in one day
of a very big life;
mine.

Amen.

Lost

I'm lost, Lord,
   I don't know where I'm going.
My life seems to have ground to a halt.
I've got no direction,
   lost the map,
   broken the compass.
Help!

Lord,
   I look ahead,
   at what my future holds,
   and I don't see anything.
I see darkness
   and confusion,
   rather than light
   and order.

It'd be great to know
   what was round the next corner,
   but I don't.
I haven't got a clue.

I'm just drifting, Lord,
   hoping that soon,
   almost by accident,
   everything that I'm doing
   will make complete and utter sense.
That's not going to happen, is it, Lord?

Did you ever feel lost, Lord?
Did you ever wonder where you were going?
Did your future ever seem confused, clouded over?

I can't see a way ahead, Lord.
I'm supposed to know where I'm going,
   to be able to make decisions about it,
   to learn things to achieve it.
It seems an impossible task.

Do you have a plan for me, Lord?
One that will make sense of who
   and what
   I am?
Can I see it sometime, Lord?
Thanks.

Amen.

Love machine

Lord,
   I'm in love!
Remember you-know-who?
Well,
   we went out,
   chatted,
   walked around a bit,
   chatted,
   sat down,
   chatted,
   then snogged!
Full on, get down and boogy
   SNOGGING!
Yeeeesssss!

It was
   THE BEST,
   Lord.
Tongues and stuff.
Totally magical.
I went all tingly.

I can't believe it's happened!
I want to smile for ever
   and then keep smiling.
I want to jump up and down
   and run about

and shout
and scream
and yell.
This is just the best feeling ever!

Will it last long . . .
I don't know, Lord.
I'm not exactly
    looking for a life-time commitment.
But at the same time,
    this is so great,
    so much fun,
    so exciting,
    that I don't want it to end!
I want it to feel like that first kiss
    for ever!
I want a first-kiss-for-ever, Lord.
A for-ever
    where I tingle all over
    and don't stop smiling.

Life's great, Lord!
I'M IN LOVE!
BRILLIANT!

Amen.

Picked last

I hate PE, Lord.
It's rubbish.
I always get picked last
   for everything.
I'm no good at any of it.
I'm not one of the 'in' crowd
   who are great at everything,
   who can run, throw, kick, lob,
   jump, sprint, hit, stop, dive,
   catch, spin, dunk . . .
I'm not one of them, Lord.

I'm one of the ones who go,
   'I've got it . . . oh, er, no . . . sorry.'
My PE lessons are nothing more
   than a space in my week
   where I wear less clothes
   and wish I were dead.
And as for cross-country running . . .

Lord, did you ever do PE?
Our teacher's a psycho.
Completely insane.
And seems to think that there are only
   four or five in his class.
The rest of us simply aren't worthy
   of his attention.

I'd love to tell him
   exactly what to do
   with his javelin.

Oh, look, Lord;
   I'm last to be picked again.
How utterly surprising.
Can you make this lesson go quicker, Lord?
Speed it up a bit?
Amazing – I'm sure I just heard you say
   'yes' and 'no' at the same time.

OK, Lord,
   here goes.
The match has started
   and I'm happily in a position
   where my very existence
   can cause the least damage.

Perhaps, Lord,
   this is nothing more than a lesson
   in what I don't want my life to become.
After all,
   I don't want to be up there with the ones
   who are always best at this and that
   and love being told.
And neither do I want to be in the middle;
   happy to bathe in someone else's glory.
And I certainly don't want to be back here
   with little or no effect.
I want to be original, Lord.

Different.
And to prove my point
    I might play the rest of this game
    standing on my head.
Do you think anyone will notice?

Amen.

So-called friends

Lord,
    I've been crying.
Today,
    at school,
    I don't know why,
    but suddenly I was the butt of everyone's jokes.
I was picked on,
    laughed at,
    pushed,
    spat at,
    joked about.
I don't know why it started,
    what caused it,
    but it happened
    and I don't want to go back.

The worst thing, Lord,
    is that some of them were people I thought
    were friends.
Not now though, Lord.
How can friends do what they did?
It doesn't make sense.
I feel betrayed.

Where do I go from here, Lord?
I don't know what to do.
I can't tell anyone really,

because there's nothing much to tell.
And I know I've got to go back to school.

I feel scared, Lord.
I didn't realise life would be this unpredictable.
I didn't think friends could turn so quickly
    and for no reason.
Just because someone starts a joke,
    why does everyone decide to join in?

It hurts, Lord,
    deep down.
I suddenly feel really lonely,
    really helpless,
    really awful.

Sit with me, Lord.

Amen.

Pressure

Lord,
   my head's about to burst
   and my eyes could well fly out
   with a resounding 'pop'
   and hit my bedroom window.

I can't do this any more, Lord.
I can't sit here,
   revising
   and revising
   and revising
   for yet more exams.

Aren't these supposed to be the best years of my life?
If so,
   then why do I have to spend them here,
   sitting behind a desk,
   trying to cope with the mounting pressure
   of needing to achieve now
   so that in a few years
   I can hopefully have a decent job?

In some ways that makes sense.
I don't want to fail.
I want to do well.
But at the same time,
   if this is the only way to do it,
   I'm not sure I can.

I had a thought the other day,
    about primary school.
Not that long ago really, is it?
And life was a little bit different then.
The most pressure I seemed to deal with then
    was whether or not
    I should have fish fingers and beans and chips
    or sausage beans and chips
    for dinner.
Hardly life-changing decisions there.

Playtime was all about play,
    not worrying about the next lesson,
    that week's homework,
    or what the results of my mocks were.

I'm not saying I enjoyed primary school,
    just that the difference between then and now
    is almost too huge for me to deal with.
I don't feel that different.
I'm taller,
    I've got more spots,
    more posters
    and more worries.

I don't remember being warned about this bit.
No one said that once I became a teenager
    I'd become very stressed
    and feel under pressure to achieve, achieve, achieve.
And I'm supposed to now know
    what I want to do next year as well!

Lord, I haven't a clue!
I'm too worried about this essay
    that next year seems a lifetime away.

I wish it was.

Lord,
    sometimes the pressure gets too much,
    makes me want to jack it in,
    give up,
    run away.
But if I did that
    I'd be even more annoyed.
I don't want to give up,
    I don't want to fail,
    and I don't want to lose sight of who and what I am either.

Help me get the balance right, Lord.
Help me make sense of all this,
    to control the pressure,
    to make sure that I play as hard
    as I work.

Amen.

Who am I?

Look at me, Lord . . .
   (yeah, it's me again).
I look . . .
   yuk.
What can I say, really?
I have the body
   I didn't ask for.
I wouldn't wish looking like this
   on anyone.
Better put a T-shirt on
   before I get too obsessed.

I hate the way I look, Lord.
I hate my body –
   it's put together all wrong.
Or something.
How am I ever going to pull with a body
   like this?

It doesn't seem fair, Lord.
Loads of people at school
   seem to be blessed
   with the physique of perfection.
Except me.
I'm blessed with . . . with . . .
   with, well what I've got.
Which isn't much really, is it?

I know it's what's on the inside that counts,
   but I think I need to impress a little first
   to make someone want to look deeper, don't you?

I've thought about dieting,
   running,
   joining a gym . . .
   all a lot of effort really.
But I've got to do something, haven't I?
   I mean . . . just look at me!
HIDEOUS!

Am I taking this a little too seriously, Lord?
Do I sound obsessed?
That's the last thing I want.
I guess I'm just concerned, Lord.
Not completely happy with who I am.
It was a lot easier when I was younger
   when as far as I was concerned, my body
   was just somewhere else
   to cover in mud.

Now, Lord,
   it's different.
I'm suddenly very aware of my body
   and what it is
   and what it does
   and what it can do,
   if you know what I mean.
I want to be happy with what I've got,

be confident in it.
It's the only body I've got
   so I'd better get used to it.

I never thought I'd feel like this, Lord.
I never realised
   I'd suddenly be wondering
   about why bits of me
   look the way they do.
It's odd
   and takes a bit of getting used to.
Being really aware of yourself
   is really strange.
There's no warning.
It's just wake up one morning and
   Wow!
   Who IS that?!?!

And, Lord,
   as I try to deal with the 'who'
   that I've realised I am
   and the 'what' this 'who' looks like,
   help me to learn
   to just keep a little hold
   on reality
   and not become obsessed.
A reflection's one thing, Lord,
   and being unhappy with it now and again
   isn't a bad thing –
   at least I might stay healthy.

But seeing that reflection
    and desperately wanting to see another in its place
    and doing anything to get it?
Not good, Lord.
Not good.

This is me, Lord.
Who I am.
How I look.
What I 'be'.
But perhaps, Lord,
    the exciting thing,
    is what I'll become.

Amen.

Self-image

I hate the way I look, Lord.
My body's just not nice at all.
It all looks wrong,
   like I was put together in the wrong order.

I want to have a body to be proud of, Lord.
I want to look good in what I wear.
I want to be able to impress people
   as well as myself,
      to feel confident in the way I look.

Is that bad, Lord?
Is that vanity?
I guess so, but I also think you understand.
I do want all those things, Lord,
   but, deep down,
   what I really want,
   is just to feel happy with who I am.
And, to a degree,
   that includes how I look.

Some people seem to look great naturally.
No effort involved whatsoever.
I envy that.
Me? I think I'm going to have to work at it a little.
A bit of running,
   watching what I eat,
   that kind of thing.

That's not a bad thing, is it, Lord?
After all, you gave me this body,
   and it's the only one I've got.
I want to look after it,
   keep it in good working order
   and in the process
   help it to look good –
   but at the same time
   not lose sight
   of the really important things in life.

Looking good is one thing, Lord,
   but there's so much else to think about,
   to be thankful for.
Perhaps you could help me focus on them occasionally,
   and stop me mirror-gazing and wishing to be
   something I'm not?

Thanks, Lord.

Amen.

Sex

Lord,
    we went too far.
Last night,
    we did things we both knew we weren't ready for.
Things that were exciting,
    fun,
    enjoyable,
    different.
It felt good, Lord,
    it really did.
But today,
    I don't know.

I guess, Lord,
    that I don't know if I'm ready for it.
I don't know if I'm quite able to cope
    with what we did.
We felt so close
    but almost too close,
    like we'd jumped rather than walked.

The most difficult thing, Lord,
    is now that we've done it,
    to decide what we do next time we're together.
Do we do the same?
Do we stop?
Do we go further?
Know what I mean?

I don't want either of us to get hurt, Lord,
   and, after last night,
   it really feels like we might.
Does that make sense?
And that's my biggest worry;
   not what we did,
   but how I feel now
   and how it could make me feel later.

It's scared me, Lord.
We both discovered a part of ourselves
   we'd never encountered before.
It was scary and exciting
   and I'd be lying to say I didn't want to do it again,
   because I do.
But I'm not sure if I should.

I'm not asking for any answers, Lord,
   just your time,
   as I try to work this out.
Help us not to hurt each other, Lord.

Amen.

Smelly feet

Lord,
　my feet stink.
Mum came into my room this morning,
　yelled something about me being really stinky
　and has now come back with something
　to put in my shoes
　to take away the smell.

Here's me in the middle of my teenage years,
　worrying about what tomorrow holds,
　about what I'll do,
　where I'll go,
　what I'll become,
　and suddenly
　the most important issue of the day
　is my smelly feet.

I can't help it, Lord.
It's not like I've trained them to become smelly.
I don't dip them in really smelly stuff
　just to annoy people.
They just smell,
　that's all there is to it.

Teenage life seems to be a hotchpotch, Lord.
Greasy hair,
　spots,
　smelly feet,

sweaty armpits . . .
it's not exactly a nice picture, is it?
Hardly something everyone wants to experience.
Being a teenager can often mean just enduring
rather than enjoying life.

Is there any reason why it has to be this way, Lord?
Isn't there any way to make it more pleasant?
More hygienic?
I guess not.
Just thought I'd ask.
After all, Lord;
you've got me for ever –
smelly feet and all.

Amen.

Questions, questions, questions

Lord?
A few questions . . .
    what's all this about?
Who am I?
What am I for?
Where am I going?
What do you want from me?
What is my purpose?
What's tomorrow all about?
Do you exist?
Am I important?
Do I matter?
Will I pass my exams?
What options do I have?
What do I want to be?
What am I good at?
Will I ever know what to do?
Will I ever hear your voice?
Do doubts ever go away?
Will my parents ever understand me?
What about my A levels?
What about that homework that's due tomorrow?
Will I be famous?
Will I die before I'm old?
Will these spots ever go?
Will girls ever fancy me?
Am I fat?

Am I thin?

Should I go to that party on Saturday?

Do I have to visit Grandma?

Why do I have to go on holiday with my family?

Will I ever be allowed to stay up late?

Why is life so unfair?

Does Mum know that I tried a cigarette yesterday?

Am I supposed to know what I want to do with my life?

Why is my hair greasy?

Why am I jealous of my best friend?

Why am I rubbish at athletics?

Why am I so average?

What's the point?

WHY ME, Lord?

Amen.